W9-CAM-316

Whose Spots Are These?

Whose Is It? Science

A Look at Animal Markings—
Round, Bright, and Big

Written by Sarah C. Wohlrabe

Illustrated by Derrick Alderman
and Denise Shea

PICTURE WINDOW BOOKS
Minneapolis, Minnesota

*To my best friend, Cabot: Thanks for always being
an inspiration to me and for finding all the joy in life!
Love, SCW*

Special thanks to our advisers for their expertise:

Debbie Folkerts, Ph.D.
Assistant Professor of Biological Sciences
Auburn University, Alabama

Susan Kesselring, M.A., Literacy Educator
Rosemount-Apple Valley-Eagan (Minnesota) School District

Managing Editors: Bob Temple, Catherine Neitge
Creative Director: Terri Foley
Editors: Nadia Higgins, Patricia Stockland
Editorial Adviser: Andrea Cascardi
Storyboard Development: Amy Bailey Muehlenhardt
Designer: Nathan Gassman
Page production: Picture Window Books
The illustrations in this book were prepared digitally.

Picture Window Books
5115 Excelsior Boulevard
Suite 232
Minneapolis, MN 55416
877-845-8392
www.picturewindowbooks.com

Printed in the United States of America.

Library of Congress Cataloging-in-Publication Data
Wohlrabe, Sarah C., 1976-
Whose spots are these? : a look at animal markings—round,
bright, and big / by Sarah C. Wohlrabe ; illustrated by
Derrick Alderman and Denise Shea.
p. cm. — (Whose is it?)
Includes bibliographical references (p.   ).
ISBN 1-4048-0611-3 (reinforced library binding)
1. Camouflage (Biology)—Juvenile literature. I. Alderman,
Derrick, ill. II. Shea, Denise, ill. III. Title. IV. Series.

QL767.W64 2004
591.47'2—dc22   2004000881

Spot a clue, and see who's who.

Look closely at an animal's spots. Spots can be round, oval, dark, or light. Spots can speckle thick fur. They can cover scaly skin or the hard shell of a beetle. Spots give an animal its own special look.

Spots can work like signals that tell hungry animals to stay away. Some spots play tricks on enemies' eyes. Some spots work like a disguise.

Spots don't all look alike because they don't all work alike.

Can you tell whose spots are whose?

Look in the back for more fun facts about spots.

Whose spots are these,

4

so bright against a grassy pasture?

These are a Holstein cow's spots.

A Holstein is a dairy cow. Its spots are like your fingerprints. No two cows have exactly the same pattern of spots. Their unique spots help show who's who.

Fun fact: A Holstein has so many spots, it's hard to tell if the cow is white with black spots or black with white spots.

6

Whose spots are these,
flashing beneath a flower's leaf?

7

These are a ladybug's spots.

Aren't they pretty? They also have an important job. The bold black spots and red color are easy for predators to recognize. The spots act as a warning to hungry animals that ladybugs don't taste good.

Fun fact: There are almost 5,000 kinds of ladybugs. Some are black with red spots. Some are white with black spots. Some have no spots at all.

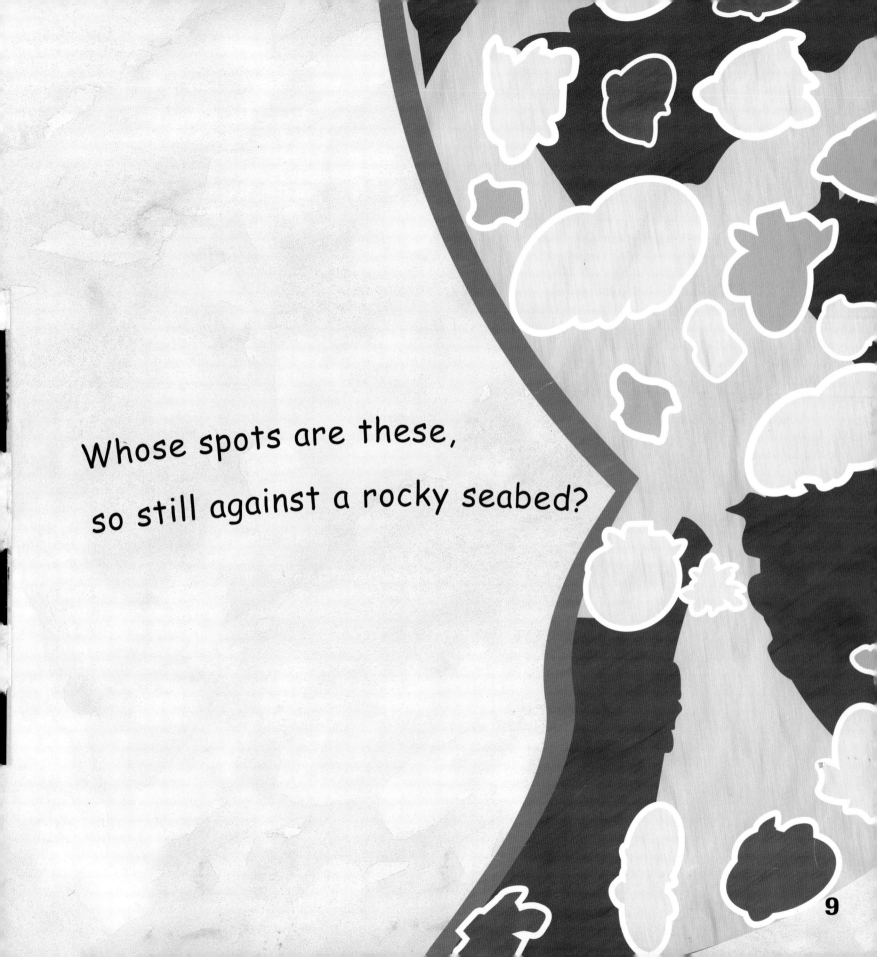

Whose spots are these,
so still against a rocky seabed?

These are a spotted wobbegong shark's spots.

This strange shark's spots give it camouflage as it lies among the rocks and sea plants on the ocean floor. Animals swimming by don't see the still shark beneath them. They swim right by its mouth. *Snap!*

The slow-moving wobbegong grabs its meal without leaving its place.

Fun fact: A spotted wobbegong also has flaps of skin around its mouth that look like seaweed. These flaps fool plant-eating creatures into coming closer.

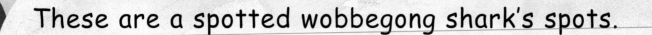

Whose spots are these, peering out from a bamboo forest?

These are a giant panda bear's spots.

The panda's spots around its eyes and ears look the same. This helps the panda hide from predators by confusing them.

Fun fact: A baby panda bear's spots are circles. As the panda grows, the circles turn into ovals.

Whose spots are these, swaying in the ocean?

13

These are a copperband butterfly fish's spots.

Don't they look like big round eyes? These pretend eyes make predators mistake the fish's end for its head. A predator can't tell which way the fish is swimming.

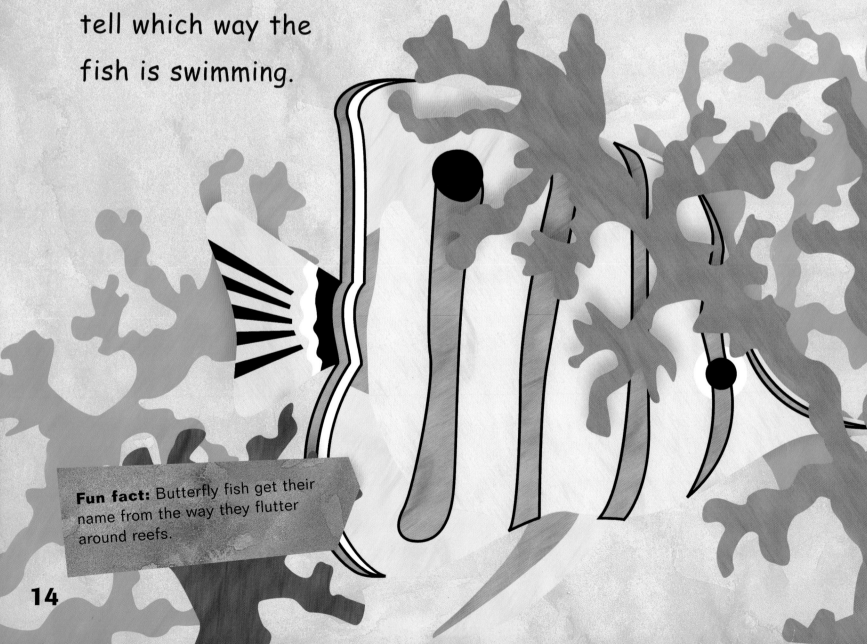

Fun fact: Butterfly fish get their name from the way they flutter around reefs.

Whose spots are these,
hiding behind a pair of ears?

These are a tiger's spots.

Cubs keep an eye on the white spots behind their mother's ears. These handy spots keep the cubs from getting lost when they follow her through a field.

Fun fact: The tiger's black-rimmed spots also may work as eyespots. Animals behind the tiger think the tiger can see them. These animals get confused and don't know which direction to run away.

Whose spots are these, fluttering in the sunlight?

These are a viceroy butterfly's spots.

With its orange color and striking white spots, a viceroy butterfly looks almost exactly like a monarch butterfly. A monarch butterfly is poisonous to birds, but a viceroy is not. Hungry birds can't tell which butterfly is which. They stay away from the viceroy just in case.

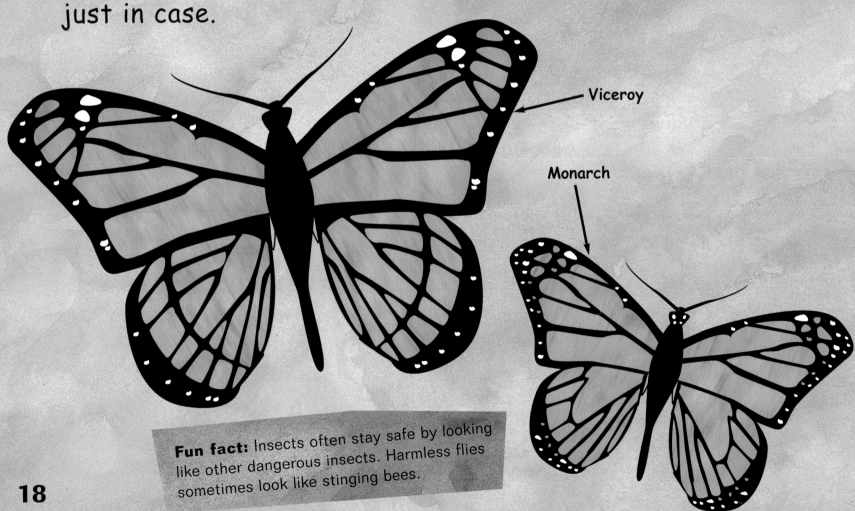

Viceroy

Monarch

Fun fact: Insects often stay safe by looking like other dangerous insects. Harmless flies sometimes look like stinging bees.

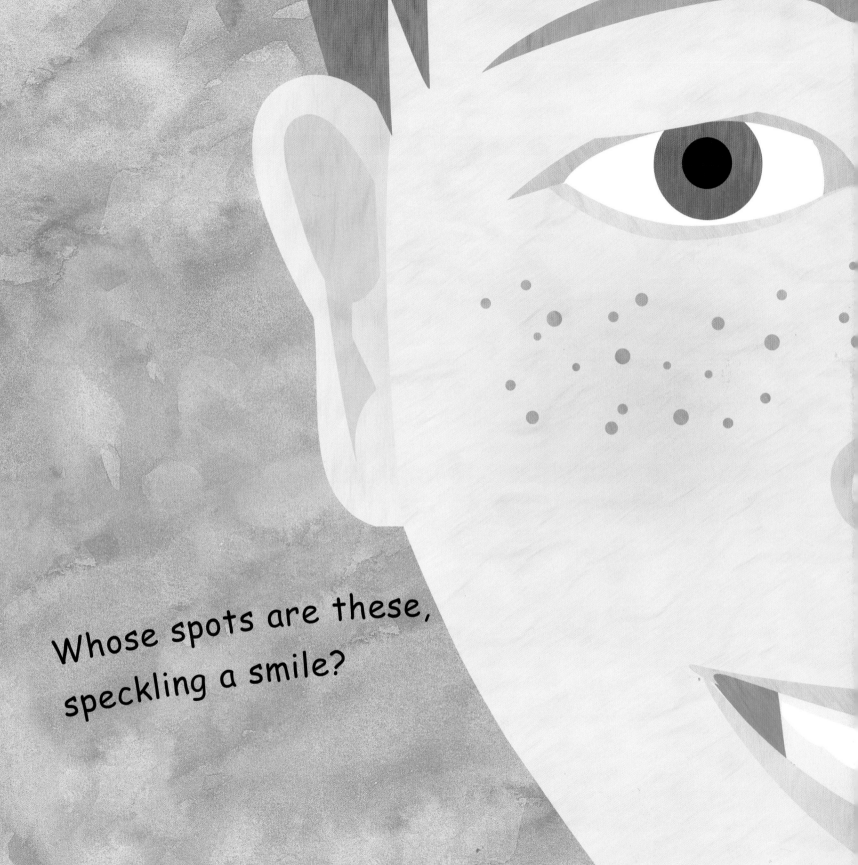

Whose spots are these,
speckling a smile?

These are your spots!

Lots of people have freckles. Do you have freckles sprinkling your nose, shoulders, knees, or toes? Can you count how many freckles you have?

Fun fact: Fair-skinned people often get more freckles after being outside. The sun makes their skin produce more melanin. That's what makes them tan. It's also what causes those extra freckles.

Just for Fun

Whose spots do what? Point to the picture
of the animal described in each sentence.

* My spots are a sign that I don't taste good.
  Who am I?   ladybug

* My spots keep predators from noticing me.
  Who am I?   panda

* My spots help keep my babies close.
  Who am I?   tiger

Fun Facts About Spots

Blurry Spots

The cheetah is a spotted cat that can run as fast as a car on the highway. That's one fast blur of spots running by!

What's in a Name?

Many animals get their names from their spots. Have you ever heard of the spotted dolphin or the spotted owl? What about the spotted dogfish or the great spotted woodpecker?

Sunlight Camouflage

Baby deer spend a lot of time curled up by plants on the forest floor. Their spotted coats make it hard for predators to see them. The deer's white spots blend in with the patches of sunlight shining through the leaves.

Always Ready for Bed

The pajama cardinalfish has a dark stripe around its middle and gold spots on its back end. This fish looks like it's wearing polka-dotted pants. No wonder it has such a funny name!

Spots to Come

A new ladybug doesn't have any spots. It takes a day or so for the beetle's spots to appear.

Words to Know

camouflage—a pattern on an animal's skin that makes it blend in with the things around it

disguise—a costume or covering that makes an animal or a person look like somebody or something else

eyespots—spots on an animal's body that look like its eyes; eyespots are for tricking an animal's enemies

melanin—a brown ingredient in skin; melanin causes suntans and freckles

oval—something that is shaped like an egg

predator—an animal that hunts and eats other animals

To Learn More

At the Library

Dahl, Michael. *Do Frogs Have Fur? A Book About Animal Coats and Coverings.* Minneapolis: Picture Window Books, 2004.

Kalman, Bobbie, and John Crossingham. *What Are Camouflage and Mimicry?* New York: Crabtree Publishing Co., 2001.

Stockdale, Susan. *Nature's Paintbrush: The Patterns and Colors Around You.* New York: Simon & Schuster Books for Young Readers, 1999.

On the Web

FactHound offers a safe, fun way to find Web sites related to this book. All of the sites on FactHound have been researched by our staff. *www.facthound.com*

1. Visit the FactHound home page.
2. Enter a search word related to this book, or type in this special code: 1404806113.
3. Click the FETCH IT button.

Your trusty FactHound will fetch the best Web sites for you!